Lead The

Way

Navigating Disruption with Innovative Leadership

Mark Mcraoph

DEDICATION

Dedicated to the visionaries, the disruptors, and the relentless innovators – those who understand that leadership is not just about steering through storms but harnessing the power of disruption to propel towards new horizons. Your unwavering commitment to forging a path of innovation inspires us all to lead the way in navigating uncharted territories with courage and creativity.

CONTENTS

ACKNOWLEDGMENTS

In acknowledgment of the collaborative spirit that fuels innovation and transformation, I extend my heartfelt gratitude to the individuals whose contributions have enriched 'Lead the Way: Navigating Disruption with Innovative Leadership.' Special thanks to the visionary leaders who generously shared their insights and the mentors who illuminate the path forward. Your collective wisdom and commitment to pushing boundaries have shaped this work and will continue to guide leaders on their journey through disruption.

INTRODUCTION

Welcome to 'Lead the Way: Navigating Disruption with Innovative Leadership.' In the ever-evolving landscape of business, leaders face a pressing reality – the disruptive force of change. This comprehensive guide is not just a manual but a strategic compass, crafted to equip leaders with the skills and strategies essential to not only weather the storm of disruption but to harness its power for innovation and growth.

As we dive into the pages ahead, we embark on a journey that explores the profound impact of disruption on leadership. Drawing insights from successful leaders who have thrived amidst chaos, we unravel valuable lessons and inspiration that transcend theory, offering pragmatic tools for real-world leadership challenges.

A central focus of our exploration is the cultivation of a culture of innovation within organizations. This isn't merely a theoretical discussion; it's a practical guide, offering actionable advice on creating an environment that sparks innovative thinking. From empowering teams to fostering collaboration and experimentation, we delve into the strategies that not only encourage change but make it a driving force for continuous improvement.

Effective decision-making in uncertain times is another pivotal theme. We dissect the challenges leaders face in disruptive environments and present strategies for making informed and timely choices. In a world where data reigns supreme, we explore the role of analytics in decision-making, providing insights on managing risk and uncertainty with confidence.

'Lead the Way' isn't just a collection of theories; it's a valuable resource. Through practical advice, real-life case studies, and actionable strategies, this book is designed to be a companion for current and aspiring leaders navigating the dynamic and often turbulent seas of modern business.

Whether you're leading a team, steering an organization, or charting your own course, the principles embedded in these pages are geared to empower you to lead with innovation and success. Let's embark on this transformative journey together – because in the face of disruption, true leaders don't just navigate; they lead the way.

1. UNDERSTANDING DISRUPTION AND ITS IMPACT ON LEADERSHIP

1.1 Defining Disruption and its Characteristics

In the dynamic and rapidly evolving landscape of today's world, the pervasive influence of disruption has become an intrinsic part of the business paradigm, impacting not only industries but entire societies. Leaders, in their pursuit of successful navigation through these tumultuous times, must comprehend the essence of disruption and its defining characteristics. At the core, disruption encapsulates a significant and often unforeseen transformation that disrupts the conventional functioning of industries, markets, or organizations. This disturbance, challenging the established norms, compels leaders to reassess their strategies, business models, and approaches. The genesis of disruption may stem from diverse sources, ranging from technological advancements and shifting consumer preferences to economic fluctuations or regulatory changes.

Delving into the intricacies of disruption unveils a set of key characteristics that differentiates it from mere evolutionary change. Central to this understanding is the acknowledgment that disruption thrives in an environment rife with uncertainty and ambiguity. The profound impact and consequences of disruptive events are inherently challenging to predict, demanding leaders to cultivate agility, adaptability, and a propensity for experimentation. Furthermore, the velocity and speed at which disruption unfolds add an additional layer of complexity. Novel technologies, ideas, and business models emerge and propagate swiftly, catching leaders off guard and necessitating a proactive stance to stay ahead of the curve.

A salient feature of disruption lies in its proclivity for radical change, dismantling established norms and practices. It possesses the transformative power to render existing business models obsolete while concurrently birthing novel opportunities. For leaders to navigate this landscape effectively, a willingness to embrace change and think innovatively becomes imperative. At the heart of disruptive forces often lie technological advancements, from artificial intelligence and blockchain to the Internet of Things. Leaders are tasked with the responsibility of staying abreast of these emerging technologies and discerning their potential impact on their respective organizations.

Power dynamics within industries and markets undergo a seismic shift in the wake of disruption. Established players may witness a dilution of their dominance, paving the way for nimble startups or new entrants to swiftly gain market share. Leaders must keenly observe these fluctuations in power dynamics and be prepared to recalibrate their strategies accordingly. Furthermore, the customer-centric nature of disruption is underscored by the evolving expectations and preferences of consumers. Modern customers demand personalized experiences, convenience, and value, necessitating leaders to prioritize customer-centricity and foster a culture of continuous innovation to meet these evolving demands.

As disruption permeates the business landscape, its impact on leadership is profound. Leaders find themselves in a landscape that demands a unique set of skills and qualities to navigate through uncertainty and rapid change. In the subsequent section, the focus will shift to the pivotal role of leadership in times of disruption, unraveling the strategies that leaders can employ to adeptly guide their organizations through these challenging and transformative periods.

In conclusion, disruption stands as a formidable force

capable of reshaping industries and markets. For leaders to effectively respond and adapt to these challenging times, a profound understanding of the characteristics of disruption is indispensable. By cultivating a mindset that embraces change, staying agile in the face of uncertainty, and fostering a culture of innovation, leaders can not only weather the storms of disruption but lead their organizations to success in a dynamically transformative world. An exemplary instance of this is evident in the tech industry, where the advent of smartphones disrupted traditional communication methods, transforming industries and consumer behaviors alike. Established players had to adapt swiftly, and new entrants like Apple and Samsung emerged as market leaders, illustrating the transformative power and impact of disruption on a global scale.

1.2 The Role of Leadership in Times of Disruption

In the dynamic landscape of disruption, effective leadership emerges as a linchpin for guiding organizations through the tumult of uncertainty and change. Leaders, equipped with the right qualities and strategies, not only navigate the challenges but transform them into opportunities for growth and innovation. The multifaceted role of leadership during disruptive times encompasses a spectrum of key attributes and actions, delineating a roadmap for success.

Foremost among these qualities is the ability of leaders to provide a clear vision and direction for their organizations amid the ambiguity wrought by disruption. This entails articulating a compelling vision that serves as a source of inspiration and motivation for teams, enabling them to focus on opportunities amidst chaos. Importantly, leaders must demonstrate the flexibility to adapt their vision as the disruptive landscape evolves, staying receptive to new ideas and emerging trends. By remaining ahead of the curve, leaders proactively shape the future trajectory of their organizations, positioning them for success.

Agility and adaptability stand as paramount virtues for leaders navigating disruption. The capacity to make swift, agile decisions and embrace change becomes imperative. Leaders must foster environments that encourage experimentation and risk-taking, nurturing innovation and continuous learning within their organizations. Recognizing that disruption necessitates strategic pivots, agile leaders navigate ambiguity with ease, making informed decisions in the absence of complete information and seizing opportunities presented by shifting market dynamics.

Resilience and emotional intelligence are indispensable facets of effective leadership during disruptive times. Leaders must exhibit resilience, maintaining composure in the face of adversity to inspire confidence and stability within their teams. Emotional intelligence becomes a tool for understanding and managing the emotions of team members, fostering a supportive environment where individuals feel valued and motivated. This emotional support becomes integral for sustaining morale and productivity amid the challenges of disruption.

Communication, marked by clarity and transparency, serves as a cornerstone of leadership during disruptive periods. Leaders must effectively communicate their vision, strategies, and expectations, providing regular updates to ensure alignment and informed decision-making within their teams. Transparency about the realities of the situation is equally crucial, acknowledging uncertainties and risks. This fosters a culture of trust and credibility, empowering teams to navigate disruption with confidence.

Collaboration and empowerment emerge as imperatives for leaders steering organizations through disruption. Breaking down silos and fostering cross-functional collaboration become essential, leveraging the collective intelligence of diverse teams for innovative problem-solving. Empowerment involves delegating authority, providing autonomy, and fostering a sense of ownership and accountability. This empowers individuals to respond swiftly to changing circumstances and seize opportunities.

Continuous learning and development form the bedrock of leadership during disruptive times. Leaders commit to staying abreast of industry trends, technologies, and best practices, seeking opportunities for professional growth. By continuously expanding their knowledge and skills, leaders bring fresh perspectives to their organizations and inspire a culture of continuous learning and improvement.

Leading by example is the quintessence of leadership in disruptive environments. Leaders must embody the qualities and behaviors they expect from their teams, demonstrating resilience, adaptability, and a growth mindset in their actions and decisions. By leading by example, leaders inspire a culture of innovation and continuous improvement, empowering individuals to challenge the status quo and contribute unique perspectives.

In conclusion, effective leadership emerges as a critical force in navigating disruption and driving innovation. Leaders equipped with the right qualities and strategies guide their organizations through uncertainty, turning disruption into opportunities for growth. Through providing a clear vision, demonstrating agility and adaptability, exhibiting resilience and emotional intelligence, fostering transparent communication, encouraging collaboration and empowerment, committing to continuous learning, and leading by example, leaders adeptly navigate the challenges of disruption, propelling their organizations toward success. A notable real-world example is the leadership of Elon Musk at Tesla, where he navigated disruptions in the automotive industry by combining a clear vision for sustainable transportation with an agile approach to technology and production. This example illustrates how effective leadership can transform challenges into opportunities, driving innovation in the face of disruption.

1.3 Adapting to Change

In the rapidly evolving and disruptive landscape of today's world, leadership necessitates an adept ability to adapt to change, steering organizations through challenges and seizing emerging opportunities. Achieving this demands a proactive and flexible mindset, coupled with the foresight to anticipate and respond to shifts in the business landscape. This section delves into strategies that leaders can employ to master the art of adaptation and guide their organizations through the dynamic currents of disruption.

At the core of these strategies is the concept of embracing a growth mindset. Leaders, by cultivating a belief in the potential for development through dedication and hard work, open avenues for continuous learning and innovation within their organizations. A growth mindset encourages a culture that welcomes new ideas, learns from failures, and consistently seeks opportunities for improvement. This foundational principle sets the stage for organizational resilience and adaptability.

Building a learning organization stands as another

pivotal strategy. Such an organization places value on continuous learning at all levels, from frontline employees to top executives. This is achieved by creating an environment that encourages experimentation, collaboration, and knowledge sharing. Leaders foster a culture where employees are not only permitted but encouraged to take risks, learn from mistakes, and share insights. This proactive approach ensures that teams are equipped with the skills and knowledge needed to adapt to change and drive innovation.

Anticipating and monitoring trends in the industry and broader business environment is a strategic imperative for leaders seeking effective adaptation. Staying informed about emerging technologies, market shifts, and changing customer preferences enables leaders to proactively identify potential disruptions and take preemptive action. This may involve investments in new technologies, development of innovative products or services, or expansion into new markets. Staying ahead of the curve positions organizations for success in the face of rapid change.

Agility and flexibility are indispensable qualities for leaders navigating change. The ability to swiftly pivot and adjust strategies in response to new information or evolving circumstances is crucial. Leaders must be willing to shed outdated practices and embrace new ways of doing things. This may entail a reevaluation of existing processes, structures, and systems to ensure alignment with the changing needs of the organization. Being agile and flexible empowers leaders to navigate uncertainty and seize emerging opportunities.

Acknowledging that adapting to change is a collective effort, leaders must empower and engage their employees in the change process. Active participation is fostered by involving employees in decision-making, providing necessary resources and support, and recognizing and rewarding contributions. By instilling a sense of ownership and accountability, leaders cultivate a motivated and resilient workforce capable of driving innovation and effectively adapting to change.

In the digital age, embracing technology and innovation becomes paramount for organizational adaptation. Leaders must not only embrace technology but leverage it strategically. This may involve investments in transformative technologies such as artificial intelligence or blockchain to streamline processes and enhance efficiency. Cultivating a culture of innovation encourages employees to think creatively and experiment with new ideas, positioning organizations at the forefront of change and ensuring a competitive edge.

Continuous improvement and evaluation form the bedrock of the adaptation process. Leaders must routinely assess their strategies, processes, and outcomes, identifying areas for enhancement and making necessary adjustments. Gathering feedback from employees, customers, and stakeholders, coupled with data analysis, allows leaders to measure the effectiveness of initiatives. This commitment to ongoing evaluation and refinement ensures organizational agility and responsiveness to change.

In conclusion, the ability to adapt to change is a pivotal skill for leaders in today's disruptive world. Through embracing a growth mindset, building learning organizations, anticipating trends, fostering agility, empowering employees, embracing technology and innovation, and committing to continuous improvement, leaders can effectively navigate change and steer their organizations toward success. The subsequent section will delve into case studies, providing real-world examples of successful leaders who adeptly adapted to change and achieved remarkable results in disruptive environments. For instance, the transformative leadership of Satya Nadella at Microsoft serves as a compelling case study, illustrating how a growth mindset and strategic technological innovation can lead to organizational resurgence in the face of industry disruption.

1.4 Case Studies

In this comprehensive exploration of successful leaders navigating and thriving in disruptive environments, we delve into case studies that exemplify innovative thinking, adaptability, and resilience in the face of formidable challenges. These visionary leaders have not merely weathered disruptions; they have strategically navigated them, providing invaluable insights into effective leadership amidst transformative change.

Elon Musk, the enigmatic CEO of both Tesla and SpaceX, emerges as a trailblazer in disrupting multiple industries. His visionary leadership has revolutionized the automotive sector through Tesla's introduction of sustainable and high-performing electric vehicles. Musk's strategic focus on cutting-edge technology, design, and sustainability has not only positioned Tesla as a pioneer but has redefined the entire electric vehicle market. Simultaneously, at SpaceX, Musk has disrupted the space industry by developing reusable rockets, effectively reducing the cost of space travel and challenging conventional norms in the pursuit of interplanetary exploration.

Satya Nadella, the transformative CEO of Microsoft, stands as another exemplar of visionary leadership. When Nadella assumed the role in 2014, Microsoft faced significant challenges in a swiftly evolving technology landscape. Under his guidance, the company underwent a remarkable transformation, embracing innovation and shifting its focus towards cloud computing and artificial intelligence. Nadella fostered a culture of innovation by encouraging collaboration, experimentation, and a growth mindset within Microsoft. This cultural shift positioned the company as a leader in cloud computing with its Azure platform, underscoring the power of adaptive leadership in the face of industry-wide disruption.

Mary Barra, the steadfast CEO of General Motors (GM), provides a compelling case study of navigating disruption in the automotive industry. Taking the helm in 2014, Barra led GM through recovery from the financial crisis and positioned the company as an innovator in electric and autonomous vehicles. Her strategic investments and commitment to customer-centricity propelled GM into the future, with the launch of the Chevrolet Bolt, an affordable electric vehicle, and significant progress in developing autonomous driving technologies. Barra's leadership is marked by a focus on fostering a culture of innovation through cross-functional collaboration and empowering employees to take risks.

Jeff Bezos, the pioneering founder and CEO of Amazon, stands as a visionary disruptor in the retail industry. Bezos' relentless focus on customer experience, innovation, and long-term thinking has transformed Amazon from an online retail platform into a global technology powerhouse. His leadership style, marked by a willingness to experiment and take risks, has cultivated a culture of innovation within Amazon. This culture has driven the company's expansion into disruptive technologies, such as cloud computing with Amazon Web Services (AWS), artificial intelligence, and robotics. Bezos' emphasis on long-term growth over short-term profits has allowed Amazon to invest strategically in new ventures and technologies, solidifying its position as one of the most valuable companies globally.

These case studies not only underscore the strategies and approaches of leaders who have thrived in disruptive environments but also highlight the dynamic and multifaceted nature of their leadership. Elon Musk, Satya Nadella, Mary Barra, and Jeff Bezos exemplify the importance of visionary thinking, adaptability, and resilience in effectively leading through profound disruption. Their experiences offer rich lessons for current and aspiring leaders on navigating challenges, fostering innovation, and strategically leading organizations in an ever-changing and competitive landscape.

2. FOSTERING A CULTURE OF INNOVATION

2.1 Creating an Environment that Encourages Innovation

In the dynamic landscape of today's rapidly changing and disruptive world, the cultivation of a culture of innovation stands as a paramount imperative for organizations striving to maintain a competitive edge. As a leader, the onus lies on you to architect an environment that not only fosters but champions innovation. This chapter embarks on an exploration of comprehensive strategies and best practices geared towards the creation of such an environment, with a focus on empowering teams, stimulating creative thinking, and instigating a culture of innovation throughout the organization.

At the forefront of this endeavor is the recognition of the critical importance of cultivating an innovative culture. In an era characterized by disruption, organizations that fail to innovate run the risk of obsolescence, underscoring the need for unlocking the full potential of teams and navigating the ever-changing business landscape. An innovative culture serves as the catalyst for inspiring employees to think beyond conventional boundaries, embrace risk-taking, and challenge established norms. It champions a growth mindset, where failures metamorphose into opportunities for learning and improvement, engendering higher levels of engagement, motivation, and a profound investment in the organization's success.

The genesis of an innovative culture invariably lies in the actions and behaviors of leaders, setting the tone for the entire organization. Leading by example becomes the linchpin, where a leader's openness to new ideas and perspectives, encouragement of the team to question existing processes, and embracement of failure as a conduit for learning collectively inspire a creative ethos. This ethos propels teams to venture into uncharted territories, fueled by a leader who takes risks and learns from setbacks, thereby instilling a culture that values experimentation.

Crucial to this dynamic is the empowerment and trust bestowed upon the team. A leader, in their pursuit of fostering innovation, must provide autonomy and freedom to the team, offering the resources, tools, and support necessary to transform ideas into reality. Trust forms the cornerstone, creating a safe space for employees to share unconventional or challenging ideas. Open and honest communication, coupled with active listening, underscores the value placed on the team's input, fostering an environment where ideas are not just heard but respected and appreciated.

Innovation, as evidenced by successful organizations, thrives in collaborative environments. Breaking down silos and promoting cross-functional teams becomes imperative, as the amalgamation of diverse perspectives and expertise leads to more innovative solutions. Initiatives such as brainstorming sessions, hackathons, or innovation workshops serve as conduits for collaboration, fostering an ethos where teamwork and collective achievements are recognized and rewarded.

The provision of resources and support emerges as a linchpin for fostering innovation. Leaders must ensure that teams have access to training and development programs, along with tools and technologies that facilitate the exploration of new ideas and experimentation with innovative solutions. A commitment to continuous learning and development becomes paramount, with encouragement for teams to attend conferences, workshops, or online courses to stay abreast of the latest trends and technologies.

In the tapestry of fostering innovation, celebration and recognition form essential threads. The successes and achievements of the team in innovative projects should be celebrated and showcased through internal communication channels. Implementation of a reward and recognition system becomes pivotal, acknowledging and appreciating innovative thinking and outcomes through monetary rewards, promotions, or avenues for career growth. Through such recognition, the significance of creativity is reinforced, motivating the team to persist in thinking innovatively.

To anchor this culture of innovation, the aspiration to create a learning organization becomes a beacon. The emphasis on continuous learning and improvement resonates at every level of the organization, with an unwavering commitment to gleaning lessons from both failures and successes. Platforms for knowledge sharing and collaboration, coupled with mentoring and coaching relationships, form the scaffolding for creating a vibrant ecosystem where innovation thrives.

Diversity and inclusion are not mere considerations but imperative components in the recipe for fostering innovation. Leaders must wholeheartedly embrace diversity in all its facets, be it backgrounds, experiences, perspectives, or ideas, creating an inclusive environment where everyone feels valued, respected, and included. Actively seeking different perspectives and challenging conventional wisdom fosters a diversity of thought, establishing an environment where individuals feel at ease expressing unique viewpoints and ideas, thereby enriching the innovation ecosystem.

As an ongoing and evolving process, the creation of an

environment that encourages innovation demands continuous evaluation and refinement of strategies. Openness to feedback from the team, coupled with a readiness to make necessary adjustments, ensures that the strategies align with the evolving needs and challenges of the organization. Leaders must stay abreast of the latest trends and best practices in innovation and leadership, cultivating a mindset of continuous improvement and adaptability. This proactive approach positions the organization not just to weather disruption but to thrive in it, laying the foundation for long-term success.

In conclusion, the creation of an environment that encourages innovation stands as a pivotal responsibility for leaders navigating the disruptive landscapes of today. Through leading by example, empowering teams, promoting collaboration, providing resources and support, celebrating innovation, embracing diversity and inclusion, creating a learning organization, and fostering continuous improvement and adaptation, leaders can instill a culture of innovation that propels organizational success. In doing so, they become trailblazers in navigating disruption with innovative leadership, leaving an indelible mark on the trajectory of their organizations.

2.2 Empowering and Inspiring Innovative Thinking

In the dynamic landscape of today's rapidly changing and disruptive world, leaders face the dual challenge of not only adapting to change themselves but also cultivating a culture of innovation within their organizations. This imperative task revolves around empowering and inspiring innovative thinking among their teams. To embark on this journey successfully, leaders must meticulously design a safe and supportive environment that becomes the crucible for creative ideation and risk-taking. This foundational step involves fostering a culture of psychological safety, where individuals feel not only encouraged but also compelled to share their ideas without the looming fear of judgment or retribution. By establishing an atmosphere infused with trust and openness, leaders can empower their teams to unleash their creative potential, explore uncharted territories, and contemplate novel possibilities.

Crucial to this endeavor is the provision of the necessary resources and support to facilitate innovative thinking. Leaders need to allocate dedicated time and budget for experimentation, furnish access to training and development opportunities, and offer mentorship and guidance. This strategic investment in the growth and development of employees serves as a tangible testament to a leader's commitment to fostering innovation, thereby inspiring teams to transcend conventional boundaries and envision groundbreaking solutions.

Encouraging curiosity and exploration emerges as another pivotal strategy in the leader's toolkit for inspiring innovative thinking. The lifeblood of innovation pulsates through the veins of curiosity and a willingness to explore new ideas and perspectives.

Leaders can catalyze this by instigating activities such as brainstorming sessions, hackathons, or cross-functional collaborations that provide fertile grounds for open dialogue and idea sharing. By orchestrating such environments, leaders can stimulate the creative faculties of their teams and kindle the flame of curiosity, motivating them to challenge the status quo.

Leaders must also champion a cultural shift in the perception of failure, viewing it not as a setback but as a natural and inevitable part of the innovation process. A culture that embraces failure as a learning opportunity becomes the breeding ground for calculated risks and invaluable insights. By encouraging experimentation and celebrating both successes and failures, leaders not only empower their teams to venture into unexplored territories but also set the stage for a mindset that views failure as a stepping stone towards success. Leading by example becomes paramount, with leaders openly sharing their own failures and the lessons gleaned, humanizing the leadership journey and inspiring teams to embrace risk-taking.

Providing autonomy and ownership forms a cornerstone in the architecture of empowering and inspiring innovative thinking. Leaders must be willing to delegate authority, entrusting their teams to make decisions and take calculated risks. This provision of a sense of ownership not only empowers employees to think creatively but also instills a proactive initiative. Opportunities for employees to work on passion projects or pursue innovative ideas further fortify this sense of ownership, enabling individuals to leverage their unique strengths and interests. By affording the freedom to explore and experiment, leaders inspire their teams to think innovatively and make meaningful contributions to the organization's success.

Recognition and reward mechanisms stand as the final strokes on the canvas of inspiring innovative thinking. Leaders must proactively acknowledge and reward innovation within their organizations through formal recognition programs, such as innovation awards or bonuses tied to innovative outcomes. Creating a culture of celebration, where innovative ideas and achievements are consistently acknowledged and commemorated, further amplifies the motivational impact. Beyond formal recognition, leaders must engage in an ongoing feedback loop, providing constructive insights and support to individuals and teams involved in innovative projects. This continual feedback not only nurtures a culture of continuous improvement but also reinforces the organizational commitment to innovation.

In conclusion, leaders, armed with a strategic arsenal of creating a safe and supportive environment, encouraging curiosity and exploration, embracing failure as a learning opportunity, providing autonomy and ownership, and recognizing and rewarding innovation, can navigate disruption successfully and propel their organizations toward success. This comprehensive approach not only unlocks the full potential of teams but also fosters a robust culture of innovation. In the subsequent section, we will delve into strategies for promoting collaboration and experimentation, further enhancing the innovative capabilities of leaders and their teams.

2.3 Promoting Collaboration and Experimentation

Leaders face a compelling mandate to foster innovation and maintain a competitive edge. Central to this endeavor is the pivotal role played by collaboration and experimentation. A leader's ability to cultivate an environment that not only encourages but champions collaboration can be transformative. Collaboration, the linchpin of unlocking a team's full potential, becomes the crucible for diverse backgrounds, skills, and perspectives to coalesce in pursuit of a common goal. This collective intelligence and creativity generate innovative ideas and solutions that may elude individual efforts. Beyond the tangible outcomes, collaboration nurtures a culture of shared ownership, accountability, trust, and respect. It fosters open communication, active listening, and the free exchange of ideas, ultimately leading to more informed decision-making and effective problem-solving.

To instigate and fortify collaboration within an organization, leaders must proactively create opportunities for team members to collaborate on projects and initiatives. This can be achieved through the formation of cross-functional teams, where individuals from disparate departments or areas of expertise converge to tackle specific challenges. By dismantling silos and promoting collaboration across the organizational spectrum, leaders lay the foundation for a dynamic culture of innovation where ideas can flourish.

Simultaneously, experimentation emerges as an indispensable component of the innovation landscape. Experimentation involves a willingness to take risks, try new approaches, and extract valuable lessons from both successes and failures. However, for experimentation to thrive, leaders must establish a safe space wherein team members feel empowered to take risks and explore new ideas without the looming specter of judgment or punishment. This necessitates the cultivation of a culture that champions learning and growth, wherein mistakes are reframed as opportunities for improvement rather than damning failures.

To create this safe space for experimentation, leaders can advocate for a growth mindset—an ethos that believes abilities and intelligence can be developed through dedication and hard work. By instilling this mindset within the organization, leaders nurture a culture that values learning, encourages risk-taking, and embraces challenges. Moreover, leaders must provide the necessary resources, including dedicated time, budget allocations, and access to tools, to substantiate experimentation. By investing in the growth and development of their teams, leaders underscore their commitment to fostering a culture where experimentation is not just tolerated but actively encouraged.

In celebrating experimentation, leaders should not merely acknowledge success but also recognize and learn from failure. Failure, an inevitable facet of the innovation process, should be celebrated as a sign of taking risks and pushing boundaries. By openly acknowledging and discussing failures, leaders contribute to creating a culture that not only supports experimentation but also builds resilience within the team, emphasizing the iterative nature of innovation.

Despite the indisputable benefits of collaboration and experimentation, barriers may impede their effectiveness. Hierarchy, communication bottlenecks, and a fear of sharing ideas are such barriers that leaders must actively dismantle. Flattening hierarchies is imperative, as these structures can stifle collaboration by fostering a sense of power imbalance and discouraging open communication. Leaders should strive to create a more inclusive and collaborative environment by promoting transparency, encouraging open dialogue, and involving team members in decision-making processes.

Psychological safety is paramount in breaking down barriers to collaboration. This safety emanates from the belief that one can take risks and express oneself without fear of negative consequences. Leaders should actively cultivate a culture of psychological safety, where team members feel not only comfortable but compelled to share their ideas, opinions, and concerns. This can be achieved by actively listening to team members, providing constructive feedback, and valuing diverse perspectives.

In the digital age, leaders should leverage collaboration tools and platforms to facilitate communication and idea sharing. Whether through project management software, virtual meeting platforms, or online collaboration spaces, providing teams with the necessary tools breaks down geographical barriers and enables seamless collaboration across teams and departments.

Encouraging interdisciplinary collaboration further enriches the innovation landscape. Innovation often flourishes at the intersection of different disciplines. Leaders can facilitate interdisciplinary collaboration by creating opportunities for cross-functional collaboration, organizing interdisciplinary workshops or brainstorming sessions, and fostering a culture that values and celebrates diverse perspectives.

To gauge and incentivize collaborative efforts, leaders should establish metrics and indicators. Tracking metrics such as the number of cross-functional projects, levels of participation in collaborative activities, and the impact of collaborative initiatives on business outcomes provides a tangible measure of effectiveness. Recognizing and rewarding collaborative efforts reinforces their importance and provides incentives for ongoing engagement.

Promoting collaboration and experimentation is an indispensable undertaking for leaders navigating the complexities of a disruptive world. By fostering a culture that values collaboration, providing a safe space for experimentation, breaking down barriers to collaboration, and encouraging interdisciplinary collaboration, leaders can harness the collective intelligence and creativity of their teams. Moreover, by measuring and recognizing collaborative efforts, leaders reinforce the importance of collaboration and create incentives for sustained engagement in collaborative and experimental endeavors. In the subsequent section, we will delve into strategies for inspiring and nurturing creativity, further enhancing the innovative capabilities of leaders and their teams.

2.4 Measuring and Rewarding Innovation

The role of innovation as a linchpin for success cannot be overstated. It serves as the driving force behind organizational growth, adaptability, and the coveted competitive advantage. As a leader, not only is it imperative to cultivate a culture of innovation within your team and organization, but it is equally crucial to implement effective mechanisms for measuring and rewarding innovative efforts. This multifaceted approach serves to not only encourage but also to motivate your team to think creatively, take calculated risks, and consistently push the boundaries of what is deemed possible. In the following exploration, we will delve into the significance of measuring and rewarding innovation, accompanied by practical strategies aimed at achieving this in a manner that aligns seamlessly with organizational objectives.

The importance of measuring innovation cannot be overstated, encompassing several pivotal facets. Firstly, it provides a means to assess the effectiveness of ongoing innovation initiatives, enabling leaders to ascertain whether they are yielding the desired outcomes. By meticulously tracking key metrics, leaders gain insights that facilitate data-driven decision-making, pinpointing areas for improvement and optimization within their innovation efforts. Secondly, the process of measuring innovation offers valuable insights into the inherent strengths and weaknesses of both individual team members and the organization as a whole. This knowledge empowers leaders to discern high-performing individuals or teams in the realm of innovation and identify those in need of additional support or resources. Armed with this awareness, leaders can efficiently allocate resources, provide targeted training and development opportunities, and bolster the innovative capabilities of their teams. Lastly, the act of measuring innovation is instrumental in communicating its value to various stakeholders, including investors, board members, and employees. Quantifying the impact of innovation on key performance indicators substantiates the tangible benefits it bestows upon the organization, garnering support and enthusiasm for future initiatives.

Identifying the right metrics is foundational to the process of measuring innovation effectively. Among the key metrics to consider, the number of new ideas generated serves as an insightful indicator of the quantity of creative ideation transpiring within the organization. This metric facilitates the recognition of individuals or teams consistently contributing innovative ideas. The idea conversion rate, measuring the percentage of ideas successfully implemented, gauges the efficiency of the innovation process, pinpointing potential bottlenecks or barriers hindering progress. Time to market, a critical metric for organizations in fast-paced industries, assesses the speed at which innovations are brought to market, enhancing organizational agility and responsiveness. Return on Innovation Investment (ROII) measures the financial returns generated from innovation initiatives, justifying the investment and guiding resource allocation. Employee engagement and satisfaction, crucial indicators of a healthy innovation culture, provide insights into the organizational environment and its impact on innovation efforts.

Equally significant is the need to reward innovation effectively, thereby motivating and incentivizing teams to sustain their creative endeavors. Recognition and appreciation stand out as simple yet potent ways to acknowledge and reward individuals or teams for their innovative contributions. Publicly recognizing achievements in team meetings or company-wide communications, coupled with personalized messages of appreciation, cultivates a sense of pride and motivation. Financial incentives, such as bonuses or profit-sharing programs, establish a direct link between innovation and individual or team performance, provided the incentive structure is fair, transparent, and aligned with organizational goals. Professional development opportunities, such as training programs or workshops, serve as valuable rewards for individuals or teams displaying a commitment to innovation. Not only do these opportunities enhance skills and knowledge, but they also underscore the organization's investment in individual growth. Promotions and career advancement, powerful incentives for consistently innovative thinkers, offer tangible career paths for aspirations and provide a clear connection between innovation and professional development.

However, it is essential to view the measurement and reward of innovation as an ongoing, iterative process rather than a one-time activity. Establishing a culture of continuous improvement and learning is paramount to the sustained success of these strategies. Regularly reviewing and refining measurement and reward strategies ensures their alignment with evolving organizational goals and objectives. Importantly, involving the team in this process by seeking their input and feedback on meaningful metrics and rewards fosters a sense of ownership and engagement, thereby enhancing the effectiveness of these strategies.

The interplay between measuring and rewarding innovation is pivotal in the realm of innovative leadership. The identification of pertinent metrics, coupled with a commitment to ongoing improvement, lays the groundwork for a culture of innovation that thrives on recognition and incentives. By quantifying the impact of innovation, leaders not only guide decision-making but also communicate the profound value it brings to stakeholders. Embracing the notion that innovation goes beyond idea generation to the realization of tangible outcomes driving growth and success, leaders can navigate the disruptive landscape with a team motivated to push the boundaries of what is possible.

3. EFFECTIVE DECISION-MAKING IN UNCERTAIN TIMES

3.1 Understanding the Challenges of Decision-Making in Disruptive Environments

In the fast-paced and ever-evolving realm of modern business, leaders grapple with multifaceted challenges in decision-making within disruptive environments. These environments, marked by incessant change, unpredictability, and the potential for unforeseen events to reshape industries, demand leaders who can make informed and timely decisions to stay ahead of the curve. Navigating through the intricacies and uncertainties associated with disruption poses a formidable task. This exploration delves into the distinctive challenges confronted by leaders in such disruptive landscapes and articulates strategies to overcome these challenges effectively.

Disruptive environments, by their very nature, embody constant change and uncertainty. Leaders operating in these landscapes must be adept at making decisions amidst ambiguity, armed with the realization that traditional decision-making approaches may fall short. Navigating through disruptive environments necessitates a preparedness to make decisions with incomplete information, take calculated risks, and embrace experimentation as a driving force for innovation and competitiveness.

A central challenge in decision-making within disruptive environments revolves around the paradox between the urgency for swift decisions and the imperative for comprehensive analysis. Leaders find themselves at the crossroads of needing to respond rapidly to evolving situations while ensuring that their decisions are grounded in a thorough understanding of associated risks and opportunities. Striking the delicate balance between speed and analysis becomes imperative to avoid impulsive decisions that could have enduring negative consequences.

Cognitive biases add another layer of complexity to decision-making in disruptive environments. These inherent mental shortcuts, while facilitating rapid information processing, can lead to irrational decision-making and inhibit leaders from considering alternative perspectives or exploring innovative solutions. Recognizing and mitigating cognitive biases is crucial for leaders to foster objective and rational decision-making in the face of disruption.

Information overload poses yet another significant challenge for leaders in disruptive environments. The inundation of information from various sources can obscure relevant insights, making it arduous for leaders to distinguish signal from noise. Developing the ability to filter and prioritize information effectively becomes paramount, necessitating the leverage of technology and data analytics. Moreover, fostering a culture of information sharing and collaboration within organizations ensures that decision-making is grounded in a holistic understanding of the dynamic business landscape.

Agility and flexibility emerge as imperative attributes for leaders in disruptive environments. Traditional decision-making processes characterized by rigid hierarchies and protracted approval cycles may become obsolete. Leaders must champion agility, empowering their teams to make autonomous decisions, fostering a culture of experimentation, and promoting learning from failures. This adaptability enables leaders to respond swiftly to changing circumstances and seize emerging opportunities in the tumultuous landscape of disruption.

Establishing a structured decision-making framework becomes a linchpin for leaders navigating the challenges inherent in disruptive environments. Such a framework should encompass elements like soliciting diverse perspectives, conducting thorough analysis, evaluating potential risks and rewards, and assessing the long-term impact of decisions. By adhering to a systematic approach, leaders enhance the quality of their decision-making and mitigate the adverse consequences of impulsive or biased choices.

The advent of technology and data analytics in the age of disruption offers leaders unprecedented capabilities. Leveraging artificial intelligence, machine learning, and predictive modeling equips leaders with invaluable insights for making data-driven decisions in real-time. This technological prowess becomes a key differentiator, providing a competitive edge amidst uncertainty.

Fostering a learning culture stands out as a fundamental strategy for leaders in disruptive environments. Encouraging continuous learning, professional development, knowledge sharing, and embracing a growth mindset empowers teams to make informed decisions and adapt more effectively to dynamic circumstances. By nurturing an environment that values learning and innovation, leaders fortify their teams against the challenges posed by disruptive forces.

External perspectives play a pivotal role in enhancing decision-making within disruptive environments. Leaders should recognize the value of engaging with industry experts, thought leaders, and mentors to gain fresh insights and alternative viewpoints. Actively seeking diverse perspectives enables leaders to challenge their own assumptions and biases, fostering more robust and innovative decision-making.

Decision-making within disruptive environments presents leaders with a distinctive set of challenges. By comprehending the nature of disruption, addressing cognitive biases, managing information overload, embracing agility, and leveraging technology, leaders can adeptly navigate these challenges. The construction of a decision-making framework, the cultivation of a learning culture, and the inclusion of external perspectives equip leaders to make well-informed decisions that propel innovation and success in an ever-evolving business landscape.

3.2 Strategies for Making Informed and Timely Decisions

Leaders grapple with the formidable challenge of making informed and timely decisions. The capacity to navigate uncertainty and execute effective decision-making is pivotal for success in today's intricate business environment. This exploration delves into a comprehensive array of strategies that leaders can adeptly employ to navigate the complexities of decision-making in the face of disruption.

Embracing a growth mindset stands out as a cornerstone strategy for leaders aiming to make informed and timely decisions. This mindset, rooted in the belief that abilities and intelligence can be cultivated through dedication and hard work, instills openness to learning, feedback, and novel ideas. Leaders, by adopting a growth mindset, approach decision-making with curiosity and a readiness to explore diverse perspectives, thereby enriching the quality of their choices.

In times of disruption, the imperative for leaders is to actively seek diverse perspectives as a fundamental strategy in decision-making. By soliciting input from individuals with varied backgrounds, experiences, and expertise, leaders cultivate a more comprehensive understanding of the prevailing situation. This diversity of perspectives becomes instrumental in identifying blind spots, challenging assumptions, and uncovering innovative solutions. Leaders can facilitate this by involving team members, stakeholders, and subject matter experts in the decision-making process.

A pivotal strategy for informed and timely decision-making revolves around the practice of data-driven decision-making. Leaders are urged to gather relevant data from diverse sources, ranging from market research to customer feedback and internal performance metrics, and analyze it meticulously to extract insights. This analytical approach empowers leaders to make more objective, evidence-based decisions, diminishing reliance on intuition or gut feelings.

In the realm of uncertainty, leaders should proactively develop scenarios and contingency plans to prepare for various potential outcomes. Envisioning different scenarios and understanding their potential impacts enables leaders to anticipate challenges and formulate strategies to mitigate risks. This proactive stance empowers leaders to make informed decisions even in the face of uncertainty, with contingency plans offering a swift and effective response to unexpected events or disruptions.

Psychological safety emerges as a crucial element for informed and timely decision-making. Creating an environment where team members feel secure expressing opinions, posing questions, and challenging ideas fosters a culture of openness. In such an environment, leaders can tap into a broader range of perspectives and insights, encouraging collaboration, innovation, and, ultimately, informed decision-making.

Decision-making frameworks provide leaders with a structured approach to navigate the complexities of making informed and timely decisions. These frameworks, such as SWOT analysis, decision matrices, and cost-benefit analysis, offer systematic methods to organize information, evaluate options, and weigh potential risks and benefits. By employing such frameworks, leaders enhance the objectivity and systematic nature of their decision-making processes.

Fostering a culture of experimentation becomes paramount for leaders in disruptive environments. This involves creating an environment where experimentation is encouraged, and failure is viewed as a learning opportunity. Such a culture empowers teams to take calculated risks and explore new ideas. Through this, leaders can gather valuable data, test hypotheses, and make informed decisions grounded in real-world results.

While data and analysis are crucial, leaders should also hone their intuition and trust their instincts in decision-making. Intuition, cultivated through a deep understanding and experience, complements data-driven insights. Leaders, by combining intuition with data, can make more holistic and informed decisions. Developing intuition requires continuous learning, reflection, and a willingness to trust oneself.

Effective communication stands as a linchpin for making informed and timely decisions. Leaders are urged to communicate decisions clearly and transparently to stakeholders, ensuring a shared understanding of the rationale behind the decision. Additionally, involving stakeholders in the decision-making process facilitates the gathering of valuable insights and builds support for decisions. Open and honest communication ensures that decisions are well-informed and accepted by those affected.

In a world characterized by disruption, leaders must commit to continuous learning and adapt their decision-making strategies. This commitment involves staying updated on industry trends, seeking feedback from others, and refining decision-making skills. Flexibility and a willingness to adapt become indispensable for making informed and timely decisions in a rapidly changing environment.

The art of making informed and timely decisions is an indispensable skill for leaders navigating the challenges of a disruptive world. By adopting a growth mindset, seeking diverse perspectives, embracing data-driven approaches, developing scenarios and contingency plans, fostering psychological safety, utilizing decision-making frameworks, encouraging a culture of experimentation, honing intuition, communicating effectively, and committing to continuous learning and adaptation, leaders can adeptly steer through uncertainty and make decisions that propel innovation and success.

3.3 Leveraging Data and Analytics for Decision-Making

Leaders confront an array of challenges in making decisions that are both informed and timely. The conventional reliance on intuition and experience is no longer sufficient, necessitating a paradigm shift towards leveraging data and analytics to extract valuable insights and enhance the efficacy of decision-making processes.

At the heart of this transformative approach is the concept of data-driven decision-making, a process that entails using data and analytics to inform and guide strategic choices. Leaders, by collecting and analyzing relevant data, can unravel a deeper understanding of their business environment, identify patterns, and discern trends, thus facilitating decisions founded on objective evidence rather than subjective intuition.

The advantages of data-driven decision-making are manifold. Firstly, it provides leaders with a comprehensive view of organizational performance, offering insights into areas of improvement and enabling data-backed decision-making. Secondly, it mitigates the risk of bias and personal preferences influencing decisions, fostering more objective and equitable outcomes. Lastly, this approach allows leaders to measure the impact of decisions, affording the opportunity to adjust strategies in response to real-world outcomes.

To effectively harness data and analytics, leaders must embark on a journey of identifying the most pertinent data types aligned with their decision-making processes. This necessitates a profound understanding of organizational goals, challenges, and key performance indicators, ensuring that the focus remains on meaningful insights rather than succumbing to information overload.

Once relevant data is identified, leaders must establish a robust data collection and analysis process. This may involve implementing data tracking systems, conducting surveys or interviews, or collaborating with external data providers. The collected data should be characterized by accuracy, reliability, and timeliness, ensuring the validity of the insights derived from it.

Analyzing the collected data entails employing a spectrum of analytical techniques and tools, including statistical analysis, data visualization, and predictive modeling. By interpreting the data effectively, leaders can glean valuable insights that inform their decision-making processes, steering them toward strategic choices grounded in empirical evidence.

Yet, the effectiveness of data-driven decision-making lies not only in the analysis but also in the ability to strike a judicious balance between analysis and action. Leaders must steer clear of the "analysis paralysis" trap, where an overemphasis on data analysis impedes decisive action. To ensure timely decisions, leaders should establish clear decision-making frameworks, complete with defined deadlines, decision criteria, and the involvement of relevant stakeholders.

Furthermore, leaders should contextualize decisions within the broader landscape, taking external factors such as market conditions, customer preferences, and the competitive landscape into consideration. By melding data-driven insights with contextual understanding, leaders can make decisions that are not only informed but also aligned with the organization's strategic goals.

Beyond merely informing decisions, data and analytics play a pivotal role in risk management. By analyzing historical data and identifying patterns, leaders can anticipate potential risks, thereby adopting a proactive stance in developing strategies to mitigate these risks and make more resilient decisions. Analytics also enables leaders to assess potential outcomes and consequences, conducting scenario analysis and predictive modeling to evaluate risks and rewards associated with different options.

Crucially, data and analytics support leaders in monitoring and evaluating the effectiveness of decisions. By tracking key performance indicators and comparing them against predefined targets, leaders can assess the impact of their decisions and make necessary adjustments. This iterative process ensures continuous improvement in decision-making capabilities, facilitating adaptation to changing circumstances.

However, the journey towards data-driven decision-making is not without its challenges. Leaders must grapple with ensuring data quality and integrity, necessitating the establishment of robust data governance processes to guarantee the accuracy, completeness, and reliability of collected data. Building a data-driven culture within the organization is another challenge, requiring leaders to champion the use of data and analytics across all levels, provide training to enhance data literacy, foster a culture of experimentation and learning, and recognize and reward data-driven behaviors.

The adoption of data-driven decision-making emerges as a cornerstone for leaders navigating the uncertainties of today's disruptive business environment. By collecting and analyzing relevant data, leaders can gain valuable insights, make informed and timely decisions, and effectively manage risks. However, success in this endeavor hinges on the establishment of robust data collection and analysis processes, maintaining a balance between analysis and action, and overcoming challenges to cultivate a data-driven culture. Embracing data-driven decision-making empowers leaders to steer through uncertainty and foster innovation within their organizations.

3.4 Managing Risk and Uncertainty in Decision-Making

Leaders are confronted with the formidable task of decision-making in the midst of uncertainty and risk. The efficacy of navigating through turbulent times and steering organizations toward success hinges on a leader's ability to adeptly manage risk and uncertainty. This section delves into multifaceted strategies and approaches that leaders can deploy to make informed decisions in the face of uncertainty.

At the forefront of effective risk management is the cultivation of a risk-aware culture within the organization. Leaders must foster an environment where employees feel not only comfortable but encouraged to identify and discuss potential risks and uncertainties openly. By establishing a platform for open communication and learning from failures, leaders can extract valuable insights and perspectives, contributing to an informed decision-making process. Embracing continuous improvement and adaptation becomes pivotal in such a culture, emphasizing the importance of learning from mistakes.

Integral to making informed decisions is the collection and analysis of relevant data. Leaders must cast a wide net, encompassing both internal and external data sources that shed light on market trends, customer preferences, and potential risks. Leveraging data analytics tools becomes instrumental in identifying patterns, trends, and potential risks that might impact decision-making. Ensuring the accuracy, reliability, and timeliness of the collected data is paramount, as decisions based on outdated or inaccurate information can lead to adverse outcomes.

In the realm of uncertainty, leaders can derive substantial benefits from scenario planning and contingency planning. Scenario planning involves envisaging multiple plausible futures and assessing their potential impact on the organization. This strategic approach aids leaders in better preparation for diverse eventualities, allowing the development of contingency plans to mitigate risks effectively. Engaging stakeholders and seeking diverse perspectives becomes pivotal when decisions are made in uncertain times. Involving key stakeholders not only enhances the understanding of potential risks but also fosters a sense of ownership and commitment. Seeking diverse perspectives contributes to more robust decision-making by uncovering blind spots and considering alternative viewpoints.

Balancing risk and reward is a delicate yet crucial aspect of decision-making in uncertain times. While calculated risks are essential for seizing opportunities and fostering innovation, leaders must meticulously weigh potential downsides and manage risks effectively. This involves a thorough assessment of the potential impact of different options, a careful balance between potential rewards and risks, and decisions aligned with the organization's risk appetite. By evaluating risks and rewards thoughtfully, leaders can make decisions that optimize the organization's chances of success while minimizing potential negative consequences.

The iterative process of monitoring and adjusting emerges as a necessity in a rapidly changing and uncertain environment. Leaders must establish key performance indicators (KPIs) and metrics to track the progress and impact of decisions. Regular review and analysis of data empower leaders to identify early warning signs, facilitating timely adjustments to strategies. This adaptability to changing circumstances ensures that decisions remain informed, grounded in real-time information.

Building resilience and agility is the cornerstone of effective risk and uncertainty management. Resilient leaders demonstrate the capacity to bounce back from setbacks, learn from failures, and adapt to changing circumstances. This resilience extends to fostering a culture within teams that views challenges as opportunities for growth. The promotion of a mindset of agility and adaptability empowers employees to take calculated risks and make decisions confidently in the face of uncertainty.

In conclusion, the adept management of risk and uncertainty stands as a critical skill for leaders in today's disruptive world. Strategies such as embracing a risk-aware culture, gathering and analyzing relevant data, engaging stakeholders, and balancing risk and reward contribute to informed decision-making. Additionally, the tools of scenario planning, contingency planning, and continuous monitoring and adjustment are indispensable in managing risk and uncertainty. By fostering resilience and agility within themselves and their organizations, leaders can successfully navigate through uncertainty and propel their organizations toward success in a rapidly changing world.

4. BUILDING RESILIENT TEAMS

4.1 The Importance of Resilience in a Disruptive World

In the contemporary landscape marked by constant change and disruption, the attribute of resilience stands out as indispensable for effective leadership. The capacity to adapt swiftly, rebound from setbacks, and thrive amid adversity distinguishes successful leaders from their peers. Resilience goes beyond mere survival in a disruptive world; it involves guiding others through challenging times and inspiring them to overcome obstacles. This section delves into the significance of resilience in a disruptive world and outlines strategies for leaders to cultivate this essential quality.

At its core, resilience is the ability to recover quickly

from difficulties, setbacks, and failures. It encompasses maintaining a positive mindset, adapting to change, and persevering in the face of adversity. Resilient leaders approach challenges as opportunities for growth and innovation, driven by a robust sense of self-belief, optimism, and determination. This mindset enables them to navigate uncertain and disruptive times with confidence.

The benefits of resilience for leaders in a disruptive world are multifaceted. Firstly, resilient leaders demonstrate adaptability and flexibility in their approach. They can swiftly assess new situations, identify opportunities, and adjust strategies accordingly, allowing them to stay ahead of the curve and lead their teams through uncertain times. Secondly, resilience is intertwined with high emotional intelligence, enabling leaders to understand and manage both their own emotions and those of their team members. This capability facilitates effective navigation through challenging situations, maintaining composure and making rational decisions. By demonstrating empathy and understanding, resilient leaders create a supportive and inclusive work environment that fosters resilience in their teams.

Thirdly, resilient leaders excel in problem-solving, approaching challenges with a positive mindset and seeking innovative solutions. They encourage their teams to think creatively and embrace a growth mindset, fostering a culture of continuous improvement and learning. Additionally, resilient leaders inspire trust and confidence within their teams by remaining calm and composed during times of uncertainty, instilling a sense of stability and security. Their ability to navigate challenges with grace and determination earns the respect and admiration of their team members, fostering a strong sense of loyalty and commitment.

Furthermore, resilient leaders serve as role models, embodying the importance of perseverance, adaptability, and a positive mindset through their actions and behaviors. By showcasing resilience, they inspire their team members to develop their own resilience and face challenges head-on.

While some individuals may naturally possess resilience, it is a quality that can be developed and strengthened over time. Strategies for leaders to enhance their resilience include self-reflection and awareness, building a strong support network, continuous learning and growth, practicing self-care, and embracing failure as a learning opportunity. Self-reflection involves understanding one's strengths, weaknesses, and triggers, allowing leaders to proactively work on developing their resilience.

Building a robust support network is crucial for resilience development. Leaders should surround themselves with mentors, coaches, and peers who can provide guidance, support, and diverse perspectives. Continuous learning and growth are essential traits of resilient leaders who actively seek opportunities for personal and professional development, fostering adaptability to new challenges.

Practicing self-care is another pivotal aspect, as

resilience requires both physical and mental well-being. Leaders should prioritize activities such as exercise, meditation, and hobbies to recharge and maintain a healthy work-life balance. Embracing failure as a learning opportunity is a hallmark of resilient leaders. They view failure as a stepping stone to success, encouraging their teams to do the same and fostering a culture that values resilience and innovation.

In a disruptive world, resilience emerges as a vital quality for leaders, enabling them to navigate uncertainty, inspire their teams, and drive innovation. By developing resilience through self-reflection, building a support network, continuous learning, practicing self-care, and embracing failure, leaders not only steer their organizations through disruption but also empower their teams to embrace change and achieve success. Resilient leaders are not just survivors; they are architects of a thriving and dynamic business environment.

4.2 Developing Resilient Leaders

In a world marked by incessant change and disruption, the imperative for leaders to embody adaptability, perseverance, and the ability to inspire teams through tumultuous times is paramount. Developing resilient leaders is a strategic imperative for organizations seeking not only to weather uncertainties but to emerge stronger from such challenges. Resilient leaders, by definition, are adept at effectively managing challenges, rebounding from setbacks, and steering their teams with unwavering confidence and determination. This section delves into the key qualities and strategies that facilitate the development of resilience among leaders, enabling them to thrive in the dynamic and unpredictable landscape of a disruptive world.

At the foundation of resilience lies self-awareness, a quality indispensable for leaders navigating through uncertainties. Leaders possessing a profound understanding of their strengths, weaknesses, and emotional triggers are better equipped to withstand the pressures of a disruptive environment. Through practices such as mindfulness, reflection, and seeking feedback from mentors or coaches, resilient leaders cultivate the self-awareness necessary to regulate their emotions and make rational decisions even amid adversity.

Crucially, resilient leaders embrace a growth mindset, perceiving failure and setbacks not as endpoints but as opportunities for growth and learning. By framing challenges as learning experiences and failures as stepping stones to success, these leaders inspire their teams to persevere and innovate. They actively foster a culture of experimentation and provide support for continuous learning and development.

Building robust relationships is another key quality of resilient leaders, recognizing the importance of trust, open communication, and collaboration within their teams. By creating an environment where individuals feel supported and empowered, resilient leaders establish a network of support crucial for navigating difficult times. Moreover, they encourage teams to build relationships beyond immediate circles, fostering a culture of collaboration and knowledge sharing.

Effective communication skills are deemed critical for resilient leaders, particularly during times of uncertainty and change. They adeptly convey their vision, goals, and expectations, ensuring alignment and motivation within their teams. By actively listening to team members, seeking input and feedback, and providing timely, constructive communication, resilient leaders create an environment conducive to idea-sharing, problem-solving, and trust-building.

Recognizing the importance of adaptability and flexibility in a disruptive world, resilient leaders encourage their teams to embrace change, experiment with new ideas, and challenge the status quo. Open to new perspectives, these leaders willingly adjust their strategies and plans when necessary, fostering a culture that values agility and innovation.

Emotional intelligence is identified as a cornerstone of resilience, encompassing the ability to understand and manage both personal and others' emotions. Resilient leaders adeptly recognize and regulate their emotions, facilitating rational decision-making and composure during challenging situations. Demonstrating empathy and understanding towards team members, they create a positive and supportive work environment, where individuals feel valued and motivated.

Leading by example is a characteristic trait of resilient leaders, embodying the qualities they expect from their teams. Transparent and authentic in their actions, they inspire teams to overcome challenges and strive for excellence. Taking responsibility for decisions and actions, learning from mistakes, and continuously improving, resilient leaders foster trust and credibility among team members.

Understanding the importance of self-care, resilient leaders prioritize their well-being, recognizing that effective leadership hinges on personal well-being. They engage in activities such as exercise, hobbies, and spending time with loved ones to recharge and rejuvenate. By setting boundaries and managing workloads to prevent burnout, resilient leaders ensure they have the energy and mental clarity to navigate challenges and support their teams effectively.

The development of resilient leaders is imperative for organizational success in a disruptive world. Possessing qualities such as self-awareness, a growth mindset, effective communication skills, and emotional intelligence, resilient leaders prioritize building strong relationships, promoting adaptability, and leading by example. Through the cultivation of these qualities and strategies, leaders can adeptly navigate uncertainty, inspire their teams, and drive innovation and success in the rapidly changing business environment.

4.3 Building a Resilient Team Culture

Leaders face the imperative of cultivating a resilient team culture as a cornerstone for overcoming challenges and fostering innovation. A resilient team culture is characterized by its ability to adapt, learn, and thrive amid uncertainty and adversity, fostering collaboration, encouraging experimentation, and empowering team members to take risks and glean insights from failures. This section delves into the pivotal elements of constructing such a resilient team culture, providing practical strategies for leaders to implement in their organizational contexts.

At the heart of a resilient team culture lies the concept of psychological safety—a belief that team members can take risks, express ideas, and make mistakes without facing detrimental consequences. Leaders play a crucial role in creating an environment where psychological safety is valued and nurtured. This involves fostering open and honest communication, promoting active listening, and providing platforms for all team members to contribute to discussions. Additionally, embracing diversity and inclusion, celebrating failures as invaluable learning opportunities, and encouraging a growth mindset are integral strategies for cultivating psychological safety within the team.

Promoting collaboration and knowledge sharing is identified as a key driver of innovation and resilience within a team. Leaders are encouraged to create cross-functional teams, bringing together individuals from diverse departments or areas of expertise to work collaboratively on projects. This approach not only promotes a diversity of ideas but also fosters a culture of collaboration. Providing opportunities for informal interactions, such as virtual collaboration tools, social events, or dedicated brainstorming sessions, further enhances collaboration. Recognition and rewards for effective collaboration serve as additional tools for reinforcing this essential aspect of a resilient team culture.

Empowering and trusting team members are crucial components of building resilience within a team culture. Leaders achieve this by delegating authority and responsibility based on individual strengths and interests, providing necessary support and resources, and fostering an environment where decisions are made autonomously. Offering autonomy and flexibility in approaching work tasks, along with investing in professional development opportunities, further demonstrates a leader's trust in the capabilities and potential of their team members.

The cultivation of a culture of continuous learning emerges as a fundamental strategy in a rapidly changing world. Leaders are urged to encourage a growth mindset within the team, emphasizing the importance of learning, embracing challenges, seeking feedback, and continuously improving skills. This can be complemented by offering learning opportunities such as training programs, workshops, and seminars. Additionally, promoting knowledge sharing through regular team meetings, knowledge-sharing sessions, or dedicated knowledge management systems reinforces the culture of continuous learning within the team.

Leaders seeking to navigate challenges and drive innovation in the face of constant change must prioritize building a resilient team culture. By concentrating on elements such as psychological safety, collaboration, empowerment, and continuous learning, leaders can foster an environment where teams not only navigate challenges effectively but also thrive and innovate. In fulfilling this leadership role, creating an atmosphere where team members feel psychologically safe, empowered, and supported in their pursuit of excellence is paramount. Through these efforts, leaders not only build a resilient team but also establish the foundation for long-term success in a dynamic business environment.

4.4 Supporting and Empowering Resilient Team Members

In the contemporary landscape of rapid change and disruption, the construction of resilient teams emerges as an indispensable facet for organizational success. Resilient team members, those capable of adapting, rebounding from setbacks, and flourishing in adversity, play a pivotal role in this context. As a leader, the responsibility lies with you to nurture and fortify the resilience of your team members, fostering an environment where they can develop and sustain this crucial quality. This section is dedicated to exploring multifaceted strategies and practices that empower leaders in creating a robust culture of resilience within their teams.

Cultivating Psychological Safety: The bedrock of resilient teams is psychological safety, encapsulating the belief that team members can express ideas, take risks, and make mistakes without facing adverse consequences. To instill this foundation within your team, it is imperative to encourage open communication, ensuring an environment where team members feel comfortable sharing their thoughts and opinions. Embracing diversity and inclusion becomes instrumental in fostering psychological safety, valuing different perspectives and creating opportunities for collaboration. As a leader, leading by example by demonstrating vulnerability and openness establishes a safe space for team members to take risks and learn from their experiences. Additionally, providing constructive feedback that focuses on growth and development further contributes to cultivating psychological safety.

Empowering Team Members: Empowering team members is intrinsic to building resilience, as it instills a sense of ownership and control over their work. Delegating authority and providing clear guidelines allow team members the autonomy to make decisions and find their own solutions. Equipping them with necessary resources, tools, and training, and offering guidance when needed, further reinforces this empowerment. Encouraging innovation and creativity becomes essential in fostering a culture where team members can explore new ideas, experiment with different approaches, and take calculated risks. Recognizing and celebrating achievements, regardless of scale, not only boosts morale but also reinforces a sense of empowerment and motivation.

Building Resilience through Growth Mindset: A growth mindset, rooted in the belief that abilities and intelligence can be developed through dedication and hard work, significantly enhances a team's resilience. Fostering a learning culture by promoting continuous learning and development within the team becomes instrumental. Encouraging team members to embrace challenges, seek feedback, and view setbacks as opportunities for growth reinforces a growth mindset. Creating a supportive team environment where experiences are shared, feedback is constructive, and mentorship and peer learning are encouraged further contributes to cultivating a growth mindset. Providing ample development opportunities, such as training programs and workshops, solidifies a commitment to the continual growth and success of the team.

Promoting Work-Life Balance and Well-being: Recognizing that resilience extends beyond work-related challenges, leaders should prioritize the overall well-being of team members. Promoting work-life balance involves encouraging self-care practices such as regular exercise, proper nutrition, and sufficient rest. Offering flexible work arrangements, including remote work options or compressed workweeks, supports a balance between personal and professional responsibilities. Creating a supportive environment where mental health discussions are normalized and providing resources like counseling services or mental health days contribute to managing stress and maintaining overall well-being. Leading by example by modeling work-life balance and openly discussing strategies for a healthy lifestyle establishes a culture that values and supports the well-being of the team.

In sum, by supporting and empowering resilient team members, leaders lay a solid foundation for success in a disruptive world. The amalgamation of psychological safety, empowerment, a growth mindset, and a focus on work-life balance and well-being forms the crux of building resilient teams. As a leader, your pivotal role lies in creating an environment that not only enables your team to thrive but also equips them to navigate challenges with resilience and innovation.

5. LEADING THROUGH CHANGE AND UNCERTAINTY

5.1 Navigating Change

In the relentless flux of our contemporary world, where change is an inevitable facet of life, leaders find themselves at the forefront of navigating these dynamic shifts to secure the success and longevity of their organizations. This chapter delves into multifaceted strategies that leaders can adeptly employ to not only manage change but to lead their teams through the uncertainties that change often ushers in.

Embracing Change as an Opportunity: Change, though often met with trepidation, is intrinsic to growth and progress. Leaders are tasked with not only acknowledging this inevitability but embracing it as an opportunity for innovation and improvement. Consider the example of a tech company transitioning from traditional office setups to a remote work model. Encouraging a culture of continuous learning within the team is pivotal, fostering a growth mindset that perceives change as a chance to acquire new skills. Transparently communicating the benefits of change and aligning it with the organization's vision, coupled with leading by example and demonstrating a willingness to take risks, collectively instills a positive mindset toward change.

Developing a Change Management Strategy: Effectively navigating change necessitates a meticulously crafted change management strategy, serving as a roadmap for implementation. This strategy encompasses various crucial steps, commencing with a thorough assessment of the need for change, identifying the problem or opportunity at hand. Consider a retail business evolving its operations in response to changing consumer behaviors. Creating a compelling vision for change, engaging stakeholders, and involving them in the change process are vital components. Breaking down the change into manageable phases, crafting detailed implementation plans, and prioritizing effective communication through various channels ensure a smooth transition. Continuous monitoring, evaluation, and celebration of milestones reinforce the adaptability of the change initiative.

Leading with Agility and Flexibility: In the face of a rapidly changing environment, leaders must embody agility and flexibility in their leadership approach. Staying informed about the latest trends and industry developments is paramount, guiding informed decision-making. Consider a manufacturing company adapting its production processes to incorporate sustainable practices in response to environmental concerns. Fostering a culture of innovation and experimentation encourages team members to take risks, fostering adaptability. Collaboration and the formation of cross-functional teams contribute to a diversity of ideas and solutions. Leaders, in this context, must exhibit adaptability and open-mindedness, being receptive to feedback and ready to adjust strategies as needed. Additionally, leading with empathy and emotional intelligence becomes imperative to understand and manage the emotions that may arise during periods of change.

Overcoming Resistance to Change: Resistance to change, a natural response, can pose a significant challenge to successful implementation. Leaders must employ strategies to manage and overcome this resistance. Consider the example of a healthcare organization implementing a new digital health record system. Communicating the reasons behind the change and its benefits, involving and engaging stakeholders from the outset, and addressing concerns openly and honestly are foundational. Providing ample support and resources, including training and mentoring, helps team members navigate the change successfully. Celebrating small wins along the journey serves to build momentum and foster a positive environment conducive to change acceptance and support.

These strategies collectively empower leaders to effectively navigate change, inspiring their teams and fostering success in the face of disruption. It's imperative to recognize that change is not a singular event but an ongoing process, demanding leaders to be adaptable, agile, and open to new possibilities to thrive in today's dynamic business environments.

5.2 Communicating Effectively During Times of Uncertainty

The leadership imperative of effective communication stands as a lighthouse guiding teams through unpredictable circumstances. As leaders navigate the complex terrain of rapid change, the ability to masterfully convey information, provide clarity, and instill unwavering confidence in their teams becomes paramount. Effective communication, in this context, transcends the exchange of information; it becomes a linchpin for assuaging anxiety, building trust, and nurturing a sense of stability amid the relentless turbulence of uncertainty. This comprehensive exploration delves into strategies and best practices tailored to facilitate effective communication during these challenging times.

A foundational principle underscores the need for transparent and timely communication. Leaders are not only encouraged but implored to embrace transparency by openly sharing information about the prevailing situation, elucidating the challenges faced, and delineating potential impacts on the organization. This practice goes beyond mere information dissemination; it cultivates trust and credibility, creating an environment where employees feel not only informed but also included in the decision-making process. Simultaneously, the importance of timeliness in communication is underscored. Leaders are advised to provide updates and information swiftly, ensuring that employees are kept abreast of any changes or developments. Timely communication serves as a preventative measure, staunchly warding off the spread of rumors and speculation, which, left unchecked, could precipitate heightened anxiety and a decline in productivity.

Clarity and consistency emerge as twin pillars in the realm of effective communication during times of uncertainty. Leaders are tasked with the responsibility of communicating with precision, employing clear and concise language. Jargon and technical terms, which might sow confusion, are to be avoided. Simultaneously, the clarion call for consistency resounds. Leaders are urged to deliver messages consistently across different channels, steering clear of contradictions. This commitment to consistency is not just a matter of linguistic uniformity; it is a deliberate effort to create a sense of stability and reliability in communication, a crucial anchor in the tumultuous sea of uncertainty.

The imperative of two-way communication takes center stage. Effective communication, the discourse contends, is not a unidirectional flow of information but a dynamic engagement that incorporates listening and responsiveness. In times of uncertainty, employees harbor questions, concerns, and ideas that merit acknowledgment and addressal. Leaders are called upon to create opportunities for open dialogue, actively listening to the multifaceted voices within their teams. This emphasis on two-way communication is not merely a procedural nicety; it is a strategic approach that fosters a profound sense of inclusion, empowering employees to contribute their insights and perspectives. Moreover, it positions leaders to identify and rectify misconceptions or concerns swiftly, thereby alleviating anxiety and nurturing a foundation of trust.

The narrative takes an insightful turn, highlighting the necessity for leaders to tailor their communication to different audiences within a diverse organizational milieu. Recognizing the kaleidoscope of information needs and communication preferences among individuals or groups, leaders are urged to discern and adapt their communication styles accordingly. Some employees may gravitate towards face-to-face meetings for nuanced interaction, while others may prefer the succinctness of written updates or the immediacy of digital communication. This bespoke approach to communication is not just an exercise in accommodation; it is a strategic maneuver to ensure that information is not only disseminated but also effectively comprehended and internalized by all, irrespective of their communication preferences.

Empathy and emotional intelligence emerge as indispensable qualities in the leader's arsenal during times of uncertainty. The narrative posits that leaders must not only be cognizant of the emotional impact that uncertainty can inflict upon their team members but also actively address these concerns. Empathy, characterized by an understanding and acknowledgment of the emotions of others, takes center stage. Leaders are implored to navigate the delicate terrain of emotions, recognizing and managing not only the emotions of their team members but also their own. Emotional intelligence becomes a guiding compass, steering leaders to be mindful of their emotional responses and adeptly respond in a manner that is supportive and compassionate. This isn't a perfunctory nod to emotional considerations; it is a strategic imperative to navigate the intricacies of uncertainty with emotional acuity.

Providing support and reassurance emerges as a beacon of light in times of uncertainty. The acknowledgment that employees may feel anxious or overwhelmed becomes the catalyst for leaders to extend a supportive hand through their communication. This involves a candid acknowledgment of the challenges at hand, coupled with an expression of unwavering confidence in the team's collective ability to overcome them. Beyond rhetoric, leaders are encouraged to offer tangible resources or assistance mechanisms to aid employees in navigating the uncertain terrain effectively. Additionally, the ethos of accessibility and approachability is woven into the fabric of this narrative. Leaders are urged to be not only the purveyors of information but also conduits of support, actively encouraging employees to reach out with any concerns or questions they may harbor. In essence, providing support and reassurance isn't a mere platitude; it is a hands-on approach to alleviate anxiety and coalesce a sense of stability and confidence within their teams.

The narrative unfolds further, encapsulating the idea that effective communication is not a static phenomenon but a dynamic process that must adapt as the situation evolves. The certainty that the landscape of uncertainty is characterized by rapid evolution propels leaders to be agile and responsive in their communication strategies. This adaptability involves a commitment to providing regular updates, adjusting the frequency or format of communication, and addressing emergent challenges or concerns. It necessitates an openness to feedback, with leaders poised to tweak their messaging based on the evolving needs and preferences of the team. Far from a rigid prescription, this adaptive communication approach is a strategic imperative to ensure that leaders remain not only relevant but also effective communicators throughout the flux of uncertainty.

Leveraging technology for communication is spotlighted as an instrumental component in the leader's toolkit. In the contemporary digital age, leaders have at their disposal an array of communication tools and technologies. This section implores leaders to harness these technological advancements judiciously during times of uncertainty. Whether through video conferencing for virtual meetings, collaboration platforms for seamless information sharing and updates, or instant messaging for swift and timely communication, technology is positioned as an enabler that transcends geographical barriers. This strategic utilization of technology isn't a mere nod to modernity; it is a deliberate effort to ensure that communication remains efficient, effective, and inclusive, even in the throes of uncertainty.

The narrative crescendos with a poignant call for leaders to communicate a compelling vision for the future during times of uncertainty. It asserts that articulating a clear direction and purpose for the organization becomes not just an option but a necessity. This involves communicating the organization's goals, strategies, and plans for the future with a resounding clarity. The narrative postulates that in offering a compelling vision, leaders have the potential to inspire and motivate their teams to not only weather the challenges of the present but to actively embrace change. By providing a roadmap for the future, leaders contribute to the creation of a sense of purpose and direction, a compass that provides bearings even when the path forward seems obscured by the fog of uncertainty.

The discourse paints a vivid tableau where effective communication emerges as the cornerstone for leaders navigating through times of uncertainty. By advocating for transparent, clear, and consistent communication, coupled with active listening, empathy, and adaptability, the narrative contends that leaders can foster an environment of trust and stability within their teams. The provision of support, the savvy leveraging of technology, and the communication of a compelling vision for the future aren't just strategic maneuvers; they are the building blocks that not only enable leaders to

5.3 Managing Resistance to Change

Change is an inevitable force, especially during disruptive periods. However, the journey of change is often met with a formidable opponent—resistance from individuals who find solace in the familiar or harbor trepidation toward the unknown. For a leader, adeptly managing this resistance becomes paramount to steering their team through the tumultuous waters of disruption successfully. In this comprehensive exploration, we will delve into nuanced strategies and techniques that leaders can employ to not only address but also overcome resistance to change within their teams and organizations.

Resistance to change is a deeply rooted human response, a natural inclination towards stability and predictability. Leaders must grasp that resistance is not necessarily a manifestation of negativity or defiance but a visceral reaction to the uncertainties and potential risks associated with change. Various factors contribute to this resistance, ranging from the fear of the unknown to a perceived loss of control, lack of understanding about the change, past negative experiences, and the clash with personal beliefs and values.

To effectively manage resistance, leaders are equipped with a strategic toolkit encompassing multifaceted approaches. Communication emerges as the linchpin, with the imperative to articulate the vision and benefits of the impending change. By elucidating why the change is imperative and how it will usher in collective and individual benefits, leaders can assuage fears and garner buy-in from their teams. In this communicative dance, involvement becomes a key partner. Actively engaging employees in the change process, fostering open dialogue, and incorporating their input into decision-making not only addresses their concerns but also instills a sense of ownership and value.

Change can be overwhelming, and individuals may resist if they feel ill-equipped to navigate the new landscape. Leaders, therefore, must provide unwavering support and essential resources. This may encompass additional training, mentoring, or access to external expertise, creating a scaffold for their teams to confidently adapt to the impending changes. Addressing concerns directly and providing reassurance is pivotal, as resistance often emanates from fear and uncertainty. By taking the time to listen, openly addressing concerns, and emphasizing the validity of those concerns, leaders can build a foundation of trust and diminish resistance.

Leading by example is not a mere adage but a powerful strategy. Leaders, through their actions, set the tone for the entire team. By embodying the willingness to embrace change and adapt to new circumstances, leaders inspire and motivate their teams to follow suit. The journey of change is arduous, and celebrating small wins along the way becomes a strategic pitstop. Recognizing and rewarding individual and collective efforts during the change process not only boosts morale but also sustains the momentum needed for successful adaptation.

In the realm of change management, leaders encounter common challenges that necessitate proactive navigation. The specter of lack of communication looms large, and leaders must ensure a clear and consistent communication plan to keep their teams informed and engaged. Trust, a delicate entity, can become a casualty of resistance. To mitigate this, leaders must be transparent, honest, and consistent in their communication, demonstrating an unwavering commitment to the well-being and success of their team members. Resistance may not only emanate from within the team but also from key stakeholders within the organization. Identifying and engaging with these stakeholders early on, understanding their concerns, and collaborating to address them become imperative steps in minimizing resistance.

Managing resistance to change is not a fleeting endeavor but a persistent and patient undertaking. Leaders must brace themselves for setbacks and challenges along the way, staying flexible in their approach. Continuous assessment and adjustment of strategies are crucial to effectively navigate resistance and drive successful change. In conclusion, the skillful management of resistance to change stands as a linchpin for leaders in times of disruption. By comprehending the roots of resistance and deploying effective strategies—communicating the vision, involving employees, providing support, addressing concerns, leading by example, and celebrating small wins—leaders can overcome resistance and cultivate a culture that not only embraces change but also thrives on innovation.

5.4 Leading with Empathy and Emotional Intelligence

Leaders endowed with the ability to adeptly navigate change and inspire their teams become invaluable assets. A pivotal facet of successful leadership in these challenging times lies in the capacity to lead with empathy and emotional intelligence. Empathy, characterized by the ability to understand and share the feelings of others, holds the key to forging profound connections with team members amidst the tumult of disruptive environments. Leaders, by recognizing and acknowledging the diverse emotions their team members experience—ranging from fear and anxiety to frustration—can create a nurturing space where concerns are expressed, stress is alleviated, and a sense of belonging and trust is fostered.

Concomitantly, emotional intelligence, encompassing the recognition, understanding, and management of one's own emotions and those of others, emerges as a linchpin in effective leadership. Leaders wielding high emotional intelligence navigate their own emotions adeptly, maintain composure under pressure, and make rational decisions. Furthermore, they excel in deciphering and responding to the emotional landscape of their team members, thereby nurturing robust relationships and fostering collaboration. The development of emotional intelligence involves cultivating self-awareness through reflection on personal emotions, triggers, and behavioral patterns. Actively listening to team members, understanding their perspectives, and responding empathetically further contribute to the augmentation of emotional intelligence.

Leading with empathy and emotional intelligence is instrumental in the establishment of trust and robust relationships within a team. Trust, the bedrock of any successful team, assumes heightened significance in times of disruption and uncertainty. Leaders cultivating these qualities create an environment where team members, trusting in their leader, are more inclined to be open, honest, take risks, and collaborate effectively. Actively listening to team members, displaying genuine interest in their concerns, and providing support and guidance contribute to building trust. Transparency and honesty in communication, even when delivering challenging news, foster a culture of trust, enabling team members to express ideas and opinions freely.

Inevitably, in times of disruption, conflicts and issues surface. Leaders equipped with empathy and emotional intelligence are better poised to manage these challenges. Understanding the underlying emotions and motivations of those involved, these leaders approach conflict resolution with sensitivity and fairness. Creating a safe and respectful space for all parties to express their perspectives, actively listening, and seeking common ground exemplify the empathetic and emotionally intelligent approach to conflict resolution.

Leaders who lead with empathy and emotional intelligence possess the unique ability to inspire and motivate their teams, even in the face of disruption and uncertainty. Understanding the individual strengths, motivations, and aspirations of team members allows leaders to tailor their approach to inspire and engage each individual. Providing clear and meaningful goals, ensuring team members understand their role in achieving those goals, and recognizing and celebrating achievements contribute to fostering a positive and supportive team culture. Sharing the leader's own vision and passion further inspires teams to overcome challenges and embrace change.

However, it is imperative for leaders to practice self-care in their pursuit of leading with empathy and emotional intelligence. Recognizing and managing their own stress levels, setting boundaries, and seeking support when needed are essential components of this self-care regimen. Engaging in activities that promote relaxation and rejuvenation, maintaining a healthy work-life balance, and delegating tasks when necessary enable leaders to prioritize their well-being. By exemplifying the importance of self-care, leaders not only ensure their own resilience but also cultivate a culture within the organization that values well-being and work-life balance.

In essence, leading with empathy and emotional intelligence is not only beneficial for the well-being of team members but also instrumental for the overall success of the organization. By fostering trust, building strong relationships, and inspiring teams, leaders can navigate disruption and uncertainty with resilience and innovation. Through continuous practice and self-reflection, leaders can develop and enhance their empathy and emotional intelligence, becoming effective and influential leaders in a dynamic business environment.

6. INNOVATION IN ACTION

6.1 Case Study 1: The Success Story of Apple Inc.

In this insightful case study, we delve into the extraordinary journey of Apple Inc., a company renowned for its unwavering commitment to innovative leadership amid disruptive challenges. Established in 1976 by visionaries Steve Jobs, Steve Wozniak, and Ronald Wayne, Apple initially thrived in the realm of personal computers. However, the early 2000s posed formidable challenges as the personal computer market reached saturation, prompting intense competition. Recognizing the imperative for a strategic shift, Apple embarked on a transformative journey, redefining itself and reshaping the technology landscape.

At the heart of Apple's success lies its resolute commitment to fostering a culture of innovation. Guided by the visionary leadership of Steve Jobs, the company cultivated an environment that not only embraced but celebrated thinking differently, pushing the boundaries of what was deemed possible. Jobs' iconic words, "Innovation distinguishes between a leader and a follower," underscored Apple's pervasive emphasis on innovation, evident in every facet of the organization, from product design to customer experience.

Central to Apple's triumph is its dedication to empowering and inspiring innovative thinking. The leadership recognized the paramount importance of a bottom-up approach, encouraging ideas to emanate from any echelon within the organization. By establishing a secure space for experimentation and risk-taking, Apple nurtured a culture where employees felt empowered to challenge the status quo, resulting in groundbreaking products such as the iPod, iPhone, and iPad, each revolutionizing its respective industry.

Collaboration and experimentation form the bedrock of Apple's innovation strategy. The company actively encourages cross-functional collaboration, bringing together diverse teams to work on projects. This inclusive approach amalgamates varied perspectives and expertise, yielding more innovative solutions. Furthermore, Apple fosters a culture of experimentation where failure is perceived not as a setback but as a learning opportunity, incentivizing employees to take risks and explore novel ideas.

Recognizing the pivotal role of measuring and rewarding innovation, Apple employs clear goals and metrics to evaluate the success of innovative projects. The leadership comprehends that sustained innovation demands investment and willingly allocates resources to promising ideas. In tandem, Apple implements a reward system, acknowledging and incentivizing employees contributing to the company's innovative endeavors. This reinforcement not only underscores the organizational value placed on innovation but also motivates employees to continually push the boundaries.

Apple's leadership exhibits exceptional acumen in navigating change and uncertainty, foreseeing market trends and proactively adapting strategies to stay ahead. Noteworthy is Apple's response to the disruption in the music industry wrought by digital downloads. Swiftly, Apple introduced the iTunes Store and the iPod, fundamentally transforming how people consume music.

Effective communication during uncertain times stands out as a hallmark of Apple's leadership. Consistently communicating a clear vision and strategy to employees, stakeholders, and customers, Apple instills confidence and trust in its ability to navigate challenges. Transparent and timely updates align the organization, ensuring a cohesive effort toward common goals.

Facing resistance to change, Apple's leaders adeptly emphasize the benefits of change and address concerns directly. They inspire and motivate employees to embrace change by highlighting the opportunities it presents for personal and professional growth, contributing to Apple's resilience amid evolving landscapes.

Recognizing the significance of leading with empathy and emotional intelligence, especially during uncertainty, Apple's leadership prioritizes employee well-being. Actively listening to concerns, providing support and resources, and fostering a sense of psychological safety within the organization contribute to a culture of trust and loyalty, enabling Apple to retain top talent and maintain high employee engagement.

In conclusion, Apple Inc.'s triumphant narrative underscores the transformative power of innovative leadership amid disruption. Through fostering a culture of innovation, empowering employees, promoting collaboration and experimentation, and adeptly leading through change and uncertainty, Apple consistently positions itself at the vanguard of technological evolution. The invaluable lessons gleaned from Apple's journey serve as a guiding beacon for leaders navigating dynamic and disruptive business environments, illustrating how embracing innovation and leading with empathy can inspire teams to surmount challenges and achieve extraordinary results.

6.2 Case Study 2: Elon Musk's Leadership Journey at Tesla

In this comprehensive exploration, we delve into the

extraordinary leadership of Elon Musk at Tesla, a company that has not only redefined the automotive and energy industries but has also become synonymous with innovation and resilience. Tesla, founded in 2003, faced numerous challenges in its formative years, including financial constraints and skepticism about the viability of electric vehicles. It was in 2004 that Elon Musk assumed the role of CEO and became the driving force behind the company's transformative vision. His leadership style, characterized by an unwavering commitment to sustainable energy, innovation, and audacious goals, has played a pivotal role in Tesla's trajectory.

Central to Musk's approach is the cultivation of a culture that thrives on innovation. At Tesla, employees are encouraged to embrace a forward-thinking mindset and challenge the status quo. Musk's leadership empowers individuals to contribute unconventional ideas, fostering an environment where risks are not just tolerated but celebrated as essential components of the innovation process. This bottom-up approach has led to groundbreaking advancements in electric vehicle design, energy solutions, and beyond.

Collaboration stands out as a cornerstone of Musk's leadership strategy at Tesla. Cross-functional teams are not only encouraged but essential in Musk's vision, bringing together diverse perspectives to solve complex problems. This collaborative ethos is evident in Tesla's integration of software and hardware innovations and the development of transformative features such as the Autopilot.

In acknowledging the significance of innovation, Musk has implemented strategies to measure and reward it, ensuring a culture of continuous improvement. Clear goals and metrics are set for projects, with resources allocated to support promising ideas. This approach not only fosters a sense of purpose among employees but also motivates them to contribute to the company's innovative endeavors.

Musk's leadership shines particularly during times of change and uncertainty. His ability to anticipate market trends and adapt strategies proactively has been crucial to Tesla's success. When faced with skepticism about electric vehicles, Musk unveiled the Tesla Roadster, a groundbreaking move that reshaped the narrative around electric cars and positioned Tesla as an industry leader.

Effective communication is a hallmark of Musk's leadership. He consistently communicates Tesla's vision and strategy, providing transparent and timely updates to stakeholders. This communication style has instilled confidence and trust, aligning the organization and stakeholders toward common goals, especially during critical moments like production challenges and market shifts.

In the face of resistance to change, Musk has exhibited exceptional skills in managing challenges. By emphasizing the benefits of change and addressing concerns openly, he has inspired and motivated employees to support ambitious projects, such as the Gigafactories and the development of the Cybertruck.

Elon Musk's leadership also reflects a keen understanding of the importance of leading with empathy, particularly during times of uncertainty. Actively listening to employee concerns, providing support, and creating a sense of psychological safety within the organization have contributed to Tesla's ability to retain top talent and maintain high levels of employee engagement.

Elon Musk's leadership at Tesla stands as a testament to the power of innovative and resilient leadership in navigating disruption. By fostering a culture of innovation, empowering employees, promoting collaboration, and effectively leading through change and uncertainty, Musk has steered Tesla to the forefront of the automotive and energy industries. The lessons learned from Musk's leadership journey can inspire leaders facing disruption to embrace innovation, prioritize collaboration, and navigate challenges with unwavering determination.

6.3 Case Study 3: Innovative Leadership at OpenAI

In this comprehensive analysis, we explore the dynamic leadership of OpenAI's CEO, Sam Altman, examining the strategic vision and proactive approach that have positioned the organization at the forefront of artificial intelligence research. OpenAI, founded in 2015 with a mission to ensure that artificial general intelligence (AGI) benefits all of humanity, has faced intricate challenges in the rapidly evolving landscape of AI. Sam Altman, as the CEO, has played a pivotal role in shaping

OpenAI's trajectory.

At the core of Sam Altman's leadership style is a commitment to innovation and ethical AI development. OpenAI has thrived under a culture that encourages cutting-edge research and transformative advancements in artificial intelligence. Sam Altman's leadership empowers researchers to explore unconventional ideas, fostering an environment where intellectual curiosity and exploration are valued. This commitment to pushing the boundaries of AI research has led to OpenAI's contributions to language models like GPT-3, which have redefined the possibilities of natural language processing.

Collaboration is a fundamental aspect of Sam Altman's leadership strategy at OpenAI. Interdisciplinary collaboration is not only encouraged but integral to the organization's mission. By bringing together experts from diverse fields, including computer science, neuroscience, and policy, OpenAI ensures a holistic approach to the development of AI technologies. This collaborative ethos is evident in the organization's commitment to safety research, policy advocacy, and responsible AI deployment.

Measuring and rewarding innovation is a key component of Sam Altman's strategy to foster a culture of continuous improvement at OpenAI. The organization sets clear goals and metrics for research projects, emphasizing the importance of ethical considerations and the societal impact of AI. This approach not only aligns researchers with OpenAI's mission but also contributes to the responsible and transparent development of AI technologies.

Sam Altman's leadership acumen shines particularly in navigating the challenges of the AI landscape. OpenAI has consistently adapted to the evolving nature of AI research, addressing concerns related to safety, bias, and ethical considerations. By actively participating in the global discourse on AI ethics and advocating for responsible AI practices, Sam Altman has positioned OpenAI as a thought leader in the field.

Effective communication is a hallmark of Sam Altman's leadership at OpenAI. Transparent and timely communication is prioritized to keep stakeholders, including researchers, policymakers, and the public, informed about OpenAI's mission, progress, and ethical considerations. This communication style has not only cultivated trust but has also contributed to OpenAI's collaborative partnerships with other research institutions and industry stakeholders.

In managing resistance to AI advancements and addressing ethical concerns, Sam Altman has demonstrated a nuanced understanding of the societal implications of AI technologies. OpenAI actively engages with external organizations, policymakers, and the public to address concerns, seek input, and incorporate diverse perspectives into its research and deployment practices.

Sam Altman's leadership approach also reflects a deep understanding of the importance of leading with empathy in the realm of artificial intelligence. Actively listening to the concerns of the broader community, including those critical of AI advancements, and actively seeking to address ethical challenges underscore Sam Altman's commitment to responsible and human-centric AI development.

In conclusion, Sam Altman's leadership at OpenAI stands as a testament to the power of visionary and responsible leadership in the realm of artificial intelligence. By fostering a culture of innovation, promoting collaboration, measuring and rewarding ethical considerations, and effectively navigating the challenges of AI research, Sam Altman has positioned OpenAI as a global leader in responsible and impactful AI development. The lessons learned from OpenAI's leadership journey can serve as inspiration for organizations aiming to contribute to the responsible evolution of artificial intelligence.

7. THRIVING AS A LEADER IN A DYNAMIC BUSINESS ENVIRONMENT

7.1 Continuous Learning and Development for Leaders

In the ever-evolving landscape of leadership, a pivotal factor in staying ahead is the commitment to continuous learning and fostering a growth mindset. This section delves into the imperative of perpetual learning for leaders and offers practical strategies to augment leadership capabilities.

Central to this ethos is the embrace of a growth mindset, a conviction that skills and intelligence can evolve through dedication and diligence. Leaders instill this mindset by nurturing a learning culture within their organizations. Encouraging risk-taking and learning from mistakes, they create environments where curiosity and innovation thrive. Seeking feedback becomes a cornerstone, with leaders actively soliciting insights from peers, mentors, and team members, valuing constructive criticism as a catalyst for personal and professional advancement. Establishing learning goals and championing the value of effort further fortify the growth mindset.

Continuous learning unfolds as a lifelong expedition that necessitates a proactive approach. Leaders propel this journey by voraciously reading, staying abreast of industry dynamics, and engaging with professional networks. Participation in conferences, seminars, and workshops becomes a vital avenue for insights from industry luminaries and peer networking. Leveraging online courses and embracing mentorship further enrich leaders' knowledge base. Joining professional associations amplifies the continuous learning trajectory, offering resources and networking channels.

Leaders, recognizing their pivotal role, are instrumental in crafting learning organizations, where continuous learning is woven into the cultural fabric. Leading by example, they actively partake in continuous learning and share experiences to inspire others. Allocating resources and providing support, leaders enable employees to embrace professional development opportunities. Fostering knowledge sharing becomes a priority, with leaders encouraging cross-functional collaboration and cultivating a culture of collective learning.

To ensure the efficacy of learning initiatives, leaders must evaluate their impact methodically. Collecting feedback through surveys, interviews, and focus groups becomes instrumental in understanding participants' experiences. Measurement of performance improvement, monitoring employee engagement, conducting post-training assessments, and seeking external validation through certifications contribute to a comprehensive evaluation framework.

Continuous learning emerges not just as a professional obligation but as a transformative journey. Leaders navigating disruption with confidence exemplify the symbiosis between perpetual learning and effective leadership. By championing continuous learning, leaders not only refine their capabilities but also cultivate an organizational culture that thrives on innovation and growth, thus ensuring resilience and success in dynamic business environments. Embracing the odyssey of lifelong learning becomes the cornerstone to empowering leaders and their teams for sustained excellence.

7.2 Building a Network of Support and Mentors

Leaders grapple with multifaceted challenges and uncertainties. Navigating this complexity successfully demands more than individual prowess—it necessitates the construction of a robust network of support and mentors. This section delves into the paramount significance of building such a network and provides pragmatic strategies for leaders to fortify these vital connections.

At the core of leadership resilience lies the importance of a support network. This network acts as a compass during complex scenarios, offering invaluable guidance and advice. Leaders, when confronted with intricate and uncertain situations, can turn to their network for insights and perspectives beyond their own purview. This collaborative approach aids leaders in making more informed decisions and adeptly steering their teams through challenges.

Beyond the realm of guidance, a support network provides a bastion of emotional sustenance. Leading in a disruptive environment is inherently stressful, and having a cohort of trusted individuals to lend a sympathetic ear and words of encouragement proves indispensable. This network becomes a wellspring of motivation and inspiration, serving as a steadfast reminder of leaders' capabilities and helping them stay focused on their goals.

Moreover, a network of support and mentors serves as a gateway to valuable resources and opportunities. Mentors, drawing from their connections and experiences, open doors to new ideas, potential collaborations, and avenues for career advancement. This expansive network becomes a conduit for industry insights and trends, equipping leaders to stay ahead of the curve and make well-informed decisions.

Building this strategic network demands intentional effort and a proactive mindset. Leaders can commence by identifying potential mentors and advisors—

individuals whose knowledge and qualities resonate with their aspirations. Industry events, conferences, and networking groups become fertile grounds for expanding this network, providing platforms for meaningful engagement and knowledge exchange. Formal mentoring programs and leveraging online platforms and social media further enrich the network-building process.

Yet, the endeavor doesn't conclude with the establishment of connections; rather, it necessitates ongoing nurturing and maintenance. Regular engagements, be it through coffee meetings or virtual conferences, fortify these relationships. Actively seeking feedback and advice from the network during challenges, and reciprocating by being a valuable resource to others, contributes to the symbiotic growth of the network.

Constructing a network of support and mentors is not just a pragmatic approach; it is an indispensable aspect of leadership flourishing in dynamic business environments. Intentionally cultivating relationships with those who offer guidance, advice, and support enhances leaders' decision-making prowess, provides access to invaluable resources, and extends emotional support during turbulent times. By embracing the outlined strategies and consistently nurturing these relationships, leaders lay the foundation for a robust and supportive network that significantly contributes to their enduring success.

7.3 Maintaining Work-Life Balance in a Fast-Paced World

The imperative of maintaining a robust work-life balance is paramount for leaders aiming to sustain both their success and well-being. The pressures of leadership, marked by the perpetual need for results, critical decision-making, and the turbulence of disruptive times, can be all-encompassing. However, this section delves into the consequential strategies and practices that leaders can embrace to not only endure but thrive amidst the dynamism of the business world.

Central to preserving work-life equilibrium is the unwavering commitment to self-care. Acknowledging that personal well-being is not a luxury but a necessity, leaders must carve out time for activities fostering physical, mental, and emotional wellness. Incorporating practices like regular exercise, sufficient sleep, and a wholesome diet becomes foundational. Beyond these, engaging in activities that spark joy and relaxation, be it personal hobbies or quality time with loved ones, emerges as a pivotal means of recharging and rejuvenating leaders.

In the relentless pace of the contemporary world, maintaining clear boundaries between professional and personal life becomes a strategic imperative. Leaders must assertively communicate and enforce these boundaries, setting realistic expectations about their availability outside of standard working hours. By doing so, leaders not only create a healthier work environment but also ensure that personal time is accorded the respect it deserves.

Effective leadership is not synonymous with shouldering every aspect of organizational responsibilities. Leaders need to embrace the efficacy of delegation and empowerment. By entrusting capable team members with responsibilities, leaders not only alleviate their own workload but also foster a culture of trust and collaboration within the organization. This empowerment not only contributes to work-life balance but also nurtures individual skill development and ownership within the team.

A judicious mastery of time management emerges as a linchpin for leaders seeking equilibrium. By prioritizing tasks based on importance and urgency—employing methodologies like the Eisenhower Matrix—leaders can navigate their responsibilities efficiently, mitigating unnecessary stress and overwhelm. Leveraging tools and technologies, such as calendars and project management software, further streamlines workflows and enhances organizational efficiency.

Leaders, as architects of their organizational culture, play a pivotal role in fostering a supportive work environment conducive to work-life balance. By championing flexible work arrangements, encouraging breaks and vacations, and discouraging a culture of overwork, leaders set a precedent for prioritizing well-being within the organizational ethos. This, in turn, contributes to enhanced employee satisfaction, engagement, and productivity.

Acknowledging the ubiquity of stress and overwhelm in leadership roles, leaders must incorporate mindfulness and stress management practices into their routines. Techniques such as meditation, deep breathing exercises, and mindfulness-based stress reduction not only aid leaders in staying grounded and focused but also bolster overall well-being. Engaging in activities promoting relaxation, such as yoga or spending time in nature, further fortifies the work-life balance.

Recognizing that leadership can be a solitary journey, leaders are encouraged to seek support and collaboration from peers, mentors, or coaches. Active participation in networking events, professional organizations, or leadership development programs facilitates the creation of a robust support network. Such a community provides not only valuable insights and guidance but also a shared sense of experiences and encouragement.

Work-life balance, being an ongoing process, demands periodic reflection and reassessment. Leaders should routinely evaluate their priorities, commitments, and boundaries against their personal and professional goals. This introspective practice may involve recalibrations, judiciously declining certain opportunities, or reassessing the allocation of time and resources. Regular reflection ensures leaders stay true to their values and maintain a sustainable approach to leadership.

The significance of maintaining work-life balance reverberates profoundly for leaders navigating the swift currents of the business world. By adopting a holistic approach encompassing self-care, boundary setting, delegation, time management, supportive cultural fostering, mindfulness, seeking collaboration, and regular reflection, leaders not only fortify their own well-being and effectiveness but also inspire their teams to emulate a healthy work-life balance. In this delicate equilibrium, leaders foster an environment where both personal and professional spheres thrive harmoniously.

7.4 Embracing Change and Embodying Innovative Leadership

Leaders are not merely navigators of change; they are champions who must not only adapt but wholeheartedly embrace it. This paradigm shift demands a transformation in mindset, a willingness to challenge the status quo, and an openness to new ideas, technologies, and methodologies. This section delves into the pivotal significance of embracing change as a leader and elucidates the embodiment of innovative leadership within the dynamic fabric of the business environment.

At the core of embracing change lies a fundamental mindset shift. Leaders are urged to recognize change not as a threat but as an inevitable catalyst for growth and success. Instead of fearing the unknown, innovative leaders perceive change as an opportunity for improvement and innovation. Cultivating a growth mindset becomes imperative, a belief that abilities and intelligence are not fixed traits but can be developed through dedication and hard work. This mindset empowers leaders to view challenges as stepping stones for growth, fostering an approach to change imbued with curiosity, a hunger for learning, and an innate capacity to innovate.

Yet, embracing change transcends mere acceptance; it necessitates the embodiment of innovative leadership. Pioneering leaders lead not just by accepting change but by inspiring their teams to embrace it fervently and think beyond conventional boundaries. They foster a culture where experimentation, collaboration, and continuous learning are not just encouraged but embedded in the organizational DNA.

To embody innovative leadership, leaders are tasked with fostering a culture of innovation. This entails creating an environment where ideas are not just welcomed but revered, where employees feel empowered to take risks and think creatively. It involves providing the necessary resources and support for experimentation while fostering cross-functional collaboration. Through such initiatives, leaders unleash the creative potential within their teams, propelling innovation to the forefront of organizational endeavors.

Continuous learning and development form the bedrock of innovative leadership. Leaders, understanding the paramount importance of perpetual growth, invest not only in their own development but also champion opportunities for their teams. Encouraging a learning mindset, they facilitate professional development through training programs, workshops, and conferences, ensuring that both leaders and teams stay abreast of the latest trends and technologies, fostering an environment that thrives on intellectual curiosity.

In the arsenal of innovative leaders, technology emerges as a formidable tool for driving change and innovation. These leaders, keenly attuned to emerging technologies and trends, fearlessly experiment with novel tools to streamline processes, enhance efficiency, and elevate customer experiences. Unfazed by the rapid pace of technological evolution, they leverage technology not merely as an enabler but as a catalyst for transformative organizational change.

Diversity of thought and collaboration are heralded as guiding principles by innovative leaders. They create avenues for cross-functional collaboration, actively encouraging diverse perspectives and ideas, understanding that innovation flourishes in the crucible of varying viewpoints. By fostering such an inclusive environment, leaders tap into the collective intelligence of their teams, propelling the organization toward groundbreaking innovation.

However, innovative leaders understand that failure is an inseparable companion on the journey of innovation. They encourage their teams to take risks, knowing that not every idea will bear fruit. Rather than viewing failure as a setback, they perceive it as an invaluable learning opportunity, urging their teams to glean insights from mistakes, iterate, and continuously improve. This perspective fosters an environment where innovation is not stifled by the fear of failure but thrives on the lessons it imparts.

Resistance to change, a natural instinct for both individuals and organizations, poses a formidable challenge for innovative leadership. Leaders must skillfully navigate this resistance to propel innovation and success. Communication becomes a linchpin; leaders must effectively convey the vision and benefits of change, elucidating why it is imperative and how it will usher in benefits for the organization and its employees. By involving and empowering employees in the change process, leaders can mitigate resistance, fostering a sense of ownership and commitment.

Providing support and resources is pivotal in overcoming resistance to change. Leaders must equip their teams with the necessary tools, training, coaching, and mentoring to adapt seamlessly to change. Leading with empathy and emotional intelligence becomes imperative during times of change, addressing the emotional needs of teams, actively listening to concerns, and providing reassurance. This empathetic leadership creates a psychological safety net, fostering trust—an essential foundation for embracing change.

In the tapestry of a dynamic business environment, innovative leadership assumes a pivotal role. It equips organizations with the agility to adapt to change, the vision to drive innovation, and the resilience to outpace the competition. By embracing change, embodying innovative leadership, and effectively overcoming resistance, leaders cultivate a culture of innovation, inspire their teams, and navigate the challenges of an ever-evolving world. In this embrace of change and embodiment of innovative leadership, leaders steer their organizations towards success in the dynamic tapestry of the business environment.

CONCLUSION

As we conclude our exploration in 'Lead the Way: Navigating Disruption with Innovative Leadership,' we stand at the intersection of inspiration and action. The journey through the dynamic realms of leadership in disruptive times has been both enlightening and empowering.

We've traversed the impact of disruption on leadership, drawing wisdom from the experiences of those who not only weathered the storm but thrived in its turbulence. From fostering a culture of innovation to mastering effective decision-making in uncertainty, the principles shared within these pages are not mere theories; they are tools designed for pragmatic leadership in the real world.

The call to action is clear – lead with innovation. Our focus on cultivating a culture of innovation isn't just a recommendation; it's a mandate. Empower your teams, foster collaboration, and embrace experimentation. Transform your organization into a crucible of ideas, where change is not feared but welcomed as a catalyst for growth.

Effective decision-making in uncertain times is an art, and you, as a leader, possess the palette to paint strategic masterpieces. Harness the power of data, navigate risk with confidence, and make decisions that propel your organization forward.

As you step away from these pages, remember that leadership is not about standing still in the face of disruption; it's about forging ahead. The disruptive forces reshaping our world are not obstacles; they are opportunities for innovation. True leaders don't just respond to change; they lead the way.

May the insights gained here serve as beacons, guiding you through the uncharted territories of disruptive leadership. The journey doesn't end with these words; it continues as you apply these principles, forge new paths, and inspire those around you to lead with innovation.

Thank you for joining us on this transformative journey. Now, go out and lead the way.